John O'Groats
To
Lands End

The Official Challenge Guide

A Walkers Guide

Brian Smailes

THERE IS A RACE TO RUN, IN ORDER TO WIN YOU MUST PREPARE YOURSELF TO WIN, NOT SIMPLY TO DO YOUR BEST.

Nunquam Solivagus

Top Ten series

THE YORKSHIRE DALES TOP TEN
ISBN 0-9526900-5-5

THE DERBYSHIRE TOP TEN
ISBN 1-903568-03-X

Other books

THE COMPLETE ISLE OF WIGHT COASTAL FOOTPATH
ISBN 0-9526900-6-3

ISLE OF WIGHT, NORTH TO SOUTH – EAST TO WEST
ISBN1-903568-07-2

THE NATIONAL 3 PEAKS WALK
ISBN 0-9526900-7-1

THE SCOTTISH COAST TO COAST WALK
ISBN 0-9526900-8-X

17 WALKS IN GLEN NEVIS
ISBN1-903568-05-6

THE GREAT GLEN WAY
ISBN 1-903568-13-7

THE YORKSHIRE 3 PEAKS WALK
ISBN 1-903568-01-3

THE LANCASHIRE TRAIL
ISBN 1-903568-10-2

THE LYKE WAKE WALK GUIDE
ISBN 1-903568-14-5

THE 1066 COUNTRY WALK
ISBN 1-903568-00-5

SHORT WALKS IN THE LAKE DISTRICT
ISBN 1-903568-20-X

MILLENNIUM CYCLE RIDES IN 1066 COUNTRY (EAST SUSSEX)
ISBN 1-903568-04-8

TOURIST GUIDE TO VARADERO, CUBA
ISBN 1-903568-08-0

JOHN O' GROATS TO LANDS END
ISBN 1-903568-18-8
FIRST PUBLISHED 1999
2ND EDITION 2004
CHALLENGE PUBLICATIONS
7, EARLSMERE DRIVE, BARNSLEY. S71 5HH

Brian Smailes

Holds the record for the fastest 4 and 5 continuous crossings of the Lyke Wake Walk over the North York Moors. He completed the 210miles over rough terrain on 5 crossings in June 1995 taking 85hours and 50minutes.

His most recent venture was to walk from John O'Groats to Lands End, completing it in August 2003 in 34 days. In August 2001 he cycled from Lands End to John O`Groats, a journey of over 900miles in 6days 13hours 18minutes. This involved carrying food, clothing and tent, and was completed without support between both ends.

Brian lectures on outdoor pursuit courses and between these travels extensively on walking expeditions and projects around Great Britain.

Long distance running and canoeing are other sports he enjoys, completing 25 marathons and canoeing the Caledonian Canal 3 times.

Having travelled extensively around Europe and the Caribbean, Brian has recently been writing international travel guides to enable the holidaymaker to access the world with ease and enjoy it as much as he does.

CONTENTS

PHOTOGRAPHS

ACKNOWLEDGEMENTS

In publishing this 2nd edition of John O'Groats to Lands End, I must thank the following people for their help and contribution: -

Pam Smailes for her support on the second half of the route.

Trevor Atkinson for photographs and walking with me the final 10miles into Lands End.

Graham and Daphne Stanbridge and Charles Came for walking a section of the route with me in Somerset and Cornwall.

The public who greeted me and made me welcome in their homes throughout the route and those who gave me refreshments or donations for my supported charity.

Hi-Tec UK for the 'Conquest' walking shoes able to stand up to the rigours of a 900mile expedition.

Katz & Co (Folkestone) Ltd for the new design Guardian Rucksack that was robust enough to cope with the weather, daily use and distance.

Brian Smailes has asserted his right to be identified as author of this work in accordance with the copyright act 1988. All rights reserved. No part of this publication may be reproduced, stored in a retrieval system or transmitted in any form, by photocopying or otherwise without prior permission of the publisher.
ISBN 1-903568-18-8
First Published 1999
This 2nd Edition 2004

Published by: - Challenge Publications, 7 Earlsmere Drive, Barnsley, S71 5HH
Printed by: - Dearne Valley Printers Ltd. Tel: 01709 872188

JOHN O'GROATS

INVERNESS

STIRLING

CARLISLE

LANCASTER

SHREWSBURY

CHEPSTOW

BRISTOL

TAUNTON

BODMIN

LANDS END

2

INTRODUCTION

The first 'End to End' was recorded in 1879 by Robert Carlyle, since that time, thousands have completed it in ever increasing numbers. People have attempted it on bicycles, including a penny-farthing bicycle, carried crosses, walked nude, carried doors and bricks, pushed wheelbarrows and travelled by car, wheelchair and aeroplane.

One of the more famous people to complete it is Dr. Barbara Moore in the 1960's. She was probably the person who re-awakened people to the challenge. Also Ian Botham the famous cricketer, his walk was publicised throughout the media and he raised a lot of money for charity.

John O'Groats to Lands End is a minimum of 874miles but as you cannot walk on motorways then it will be around the 900mile mark. Either way it represents a challenge that cannot be taken lightly. To complete this challenge requires dedication, commitment and a sense of purpose. Training the body to cope with the daily distance and the mind to cope with the solitude are important aspects in your preparation for this ultimate British challenge.

John O'Groats is situated at the northern tip of mainland Britain with fine views over the Pentland Firth, Britain's second busiest shipping channel, towards the Orkney Islands. There is the last house in Scotland, a tourist information centre and a cluster of recently built shops. The famous signpost there points to Lands End, and the start line, where you leave for your marathon adventure, is beside the hotel.

The name John O'Groats dates back to 1496 when three Dutch brothers, the de Groots, worked on the land and sea in that area. Eventually the area became known as John O'Groats.

Lands End is the most southwesterly tip of the English mainland. Again the central point is the signpost, which points to John O'Groats, New York and The Isles of Scilly. There is a visitor centre with attractions, shops, café and hotel. Lands End itself covers about 100acres and is an area of natural beauty. Many people visit, especially throughout the summer. The sea around Lands End is a graveyard for ships with many wrecks around it, one of the more famous and recent being the Torrey Canyon.

The journey between both points is long, can be dangerous on the road, and remote in a number of areas, so correct preparation and planning is essential if you are to complete this walk. Follow the advice and recommendations in this book then it is down to you and your ability to stay the course for 900miles.

Between April and October is obviously the best time to attempt the challenge, but the best time to go would be May/June. This is for a number of reasons: -

A. The days are long and if you are feeling fit, you can make good progress either early or late in the evening.

B. It is not usually too hot in May/June compared to July/August and you will not be left feeling exhausted because of the heat and having to drink so much to avoid dehydration.

C. Walking in May/June means you miss the main holiday time of July/August when B&Bs get booked early and there is a lot more holiday traffic on the roads. Generally it is a lot better to go in May/June.

D. Prices often rise for the main holiday months of July/August in B&Bs and for items in shops, so going earlier means you may not spend as much overall.

THE CHALLENGE

I have described to you in this book what I feel is the shortest route by road baring a few small exceptions. Generally the route is mostly on 'A' roads but ventures onto some minor roads in Scotland and Devon. The route is the main official challenge route walked by most people, and if you walk another route then you end up walking further! It usually takes between 30 and 60 days to complete the journey depending if you are a fast or slow walker or if you want a more leisurely walk, stopping off in most villages on route.

The distance of 900miles, divided into twenty or thirty miles a day may seem to some people an easy daily distance, bear in mind that you do this day in day out and that is the difficult part. Add to this the fact that you are walking on a hard surface most of the time with the possibility of injuries like blisters, swollen knees/ankles, shin splints and general chafing of shoulders and other areas, then you can be in for a hard challenge ahead.

The remoteness of some areas, particularly Scotland means that you need to carry a supply of food with you. There are shops in some villages but this often means you need to turn off your route to go into the villages, resulting in walking extra miles and taking longer for your walk overall.

Something that can present a problem is your safety on the road. Wearing something of high visibility is important, as is walking facing the traffic. These and other safety points will be looked at in detail later.

You can generally divide the route up into three sections, John O'Groats to Carlisle, the border to Bristol then the final leg to Lands End. I felt that the hardest section was the first one through Scotland due to the lack of shops and general amenities and the hills to climb on route. Devon and Cornwall presented a lesser problem because of the many small hills in the area and having to walk along the A30 in heavy traffic, it is hazardous.

I found it helpful to take a 'bivi' bag or a lightweight tent, which can be used if there are no B&Bs as often happens. I have included some B&Bs also Tourist Information Centres on route. This will help you when planning your walk.

Many people have a support vehicle to accompany them. This is good if you can find someone with the time and the vehicle to do it. An estate car where you can sleep in the back is ideal, but any vehicle will do to support you, with carrying your equipment as well as supplying you with drinks and food on route.

On a walk of this type and length you will probably lose weight. I lost nearly 1½ stone and I know others who have lost a similar amount. Eat regularly, especially when walking, usually little and often to keep your energy levels up.

Now you have an insight into the pleasures and pains on this expedition let us continue our preparation and look at the more detailed planning.

PLANNING PHASE

There are a number of aspects to this section so we will look at each part in detail.

The Route: -
You need to be familiar with the route well before you leave. There are many detailed maps on the market showing the route described in this book. I suggest photocopying only the relevant sections of the route to carry with you. This cuts down on weight and you only have the sections of the route with you that you are not familiar with. You can then discard the individual sheets, as you are finished with them.

It is easy planning to walk a set distance each day, however in practice this can quickly change. You are walking on roads and hard surfaces; blisters are common for virtually all walkers at some stage of the expedition. The soles of your feet may hurt considerably due to walking on hard surfaces or you may just be out of energy some days and cannot walk any further. While taking note where the villages are, walk as far each day as you feel comfortable with. When I walked, I found it took the first week to get used to walking on the hard surface after that some days I could walk up to 40miles a day, on others it was only 20miles.

Weather can play a big part in how far you can walk each day. I found that wearing waterproofs was helpful if I was not sweating, but generally I got wetter wearing them, so later in the walk I resolved to only wearing shorts and vest that are quick drying. The rain may have soaked me but it was refreshing and I walked a lot quicker and further.

One important point is to ensure that the air temperature is warm enough to enable you to wear the minimum of clothing otherwise you may get hypothermia. Smearing Vaseline on the legs and arms will allow the rain to quickly run off and help to keep you warmer. I can recommend this method providing you have dry clothing in your rucksack to use if necessary and you are not cold in the rain.

Clothing & Equipment: -
The months before your expedition gives you time to acquire your clothing and equipment. Whatever you buy needs to be strong and durable enough to last the length of your expedition. Above all your clothing needs to keep you warm and protected from the elements. Try to purchase light coloured or reflective clothing where possible.

Your rucksack needs to be large enough to get all your belongings inside. The size will depend on whether you are being supported or not and whether you intend to camp, use a bivi bag or go B&B. Whatever your preference, take only the essentials with you, and get them collected together well before you leave so you can see what size rucksack you need. I used a rucksack, which had large side pockets and was robust enough for daily constant use, and to stand the various weather conditions.

Every ounce or gram you carry mounts up, and soon you will have a heavy rucksack. Ensure the straps on the rucksack are wide and padded. Carrying a heavy rucksack for one, two or three days, is usually no problem, but try carrying it each day for four to eight weeks! A combination of weight, sweat and distance all take their toll and you may find your back and shoulders ache and your skin chafes badly with the straps cutting into your skin.

Take a torch, but not one that needs four or six heavy batteries, think of the weight.

Your footwear is probably the most important item. Suffer problems with your feet and you may be forced to abandon your walk. Select a pair of walking shoes, trainers or boots well before you leave and wear them around the house to 'wear them in'. Use them for doing your training walks to get used to wearing them on a hard surface.

I used two pair of Hi-Tec 'Conquest' walking shoes that were 100% waterproof and very comfortable. You can alternate the footwear every 2-3 hours as I did to relieve pressure on different parts of the feet. You may want to try sorbothane innersoles to help cushion your feet, but experiment with them before you leave home. See equipment list in 'Questions you may ask'.

Food: -
Any food you carry should when possible be in small quantities. Throughout the route there are many towns, villages and corner shops to buy food apart from the areas that are more remote e.g. in Scotland as well as along the A30 in Cornwall. These I have mentioned in other sections of the book.

Carry enough food/snacks for the days when you are walking in the remote areas. Generally there are fuel stations where you can buy snacks and occasionally you pass truck stops or roadside cafes. These places provide cheap meals and drinks, which I found very welcoming as

I walked. Try to eat food for energy e.g. fruit, nut type chocolate bars and when stopping for a full meal eat rice, pasta, wholemeal bread and jacket potato meals. Plan your route to arrive near villages and/or food stops if possible, but have some spare food in your rucksack just in case this difficult.

I did not take a stove with me, due to the space and weight. My main meals were purchased in places like Co-op or Tesco cafés, bar meals and roadside cafes/truck stops.

TRAINING PLAN

To complete a venture as long as this, requires a good level of fitness and stamina. Start your training with short walks and build up over a few months to walking 25miles a day over a three-day period (on road). You will find that any extra training you can do in the gym, swimming or jogging will all help, but do not overdo it. The two weeks before your walk ease off on the training and rest more. Use the time to sort out your clothing and equipment.

Wear a rucksack when training, with a similar weight you will be carrying and test if the straps cut into your shoulders. Become accustomed to walking carrying a heavy weight. I also carried a waist belt with two water bottles on it and a pouch in between for a camera and small items.

Wear the clothing and shoes you will be wearing on the expedition, testing them to find any problems, e.g. shoes rubbing on toes, t - shirt chaffing skin or rucksack straps hurting. Adjust or replace where possible. The more preparation you can do, not only in training but also in preparation of equipment then the better you will be prepared.

If taking a tent or a bivi bag, try erecting the tent or sleeping in the bivi bag prior to the walk to find any possible problems before you leave.

SAFETY CONSIDERATIONS

Much of this route consists of walking on roads, which can be extremely busy especially in rush hour traffic. It is very important to be aware of the hazards a walker poses to the unsuspecting driver. Try if possible to make an early start around 5.30am or earlier if you can, depending upon the time of year. This will help you to cover some distance before traffic builds up on the roads, apart from having cleaner air to breathe.

Choice of clothing is important especially the wearing of bright reflective or high visibility clothing (photo 5), similar to what the police wear. Bright clothing helps you to be seen and could ultimately save your life. I used bright yellow shorts most of the time and a bright yellow vest in hot weather or when walking on winding roads. On roads with no footpaths you must be alert at all times, walk facing the oncoming traffic. If there are footpaths on either side of the road then try to use them for your own safety.

Take a good lightweight torch, as you may need it during the night or for some other emergency. Do not try to walk on roads with no footpaths in darkness, as it is very dangerous. Use the daylight for walking.

Carry some identity with you and contact friends or relatives regularly to report your position. I found it very helpful to carry a mobile telephone with me. It can be recharged if you stay in any B&Bs. In some areas there is no reception e.g. mountainous areas and some other places. You can also use your phone if you need to phone a TIC for more B&Bs or other information.

Depending on the time of year you may need midge cream or sun cream. I found these necessary, walking in August, and especially going through Scotland, as the midges were plentiful. A good covering of midge cream and I was thankfully saved from bites. Sunglasses may be of benefit, but that is another item to carry.

Take plenty of drinks with you and refill where you can, even by knocking on doors or asking in shops you pass. If you sweat a lot you may need three water bottles, as sometimes it is quite a way between habitations, particularly in Scotland. Eat little and often during the day to keep your energy levels up, having a good meal in the evening. Carry enough food for the section, and plan ahead but do not take too much as you have to carry it.

Take a good supply of first aid items with you, particularly plasters or similar for blisters, elastic stockings for leg problems and knee/ankle supports. A tube of anti-histamine cream for nettle or wasp stings is very useful as I found out. A supply of anti-inflammatory tablets can be of use if you are accustomed to swelling of various joints.

Summarising this section, the most important points to consider are the wearing of bright clothing, having plenty of water to avoid dehydration and blister treatments.

PUBLICITY & SPONSORSHIP

In events of this kind it is not just the challenge of completing the walk but to raise sponsorship for a worthwhile cause. There are many charities that will produce sponsorship forms for you to circulate among friends etc. This can bring in sometimes thousands of pounds for the charity of your choice.

An alternative to the well-used sponsor form is guessing your finishing time forms. People can guess when you will finish in days, hours, minutes and seconds from the start line to the finish line. It is of course pure guesswork and you could charge per guess.

Asking companies for donations is worth considering if you are having a support vehicle and you are prepared to advertise their company on the vehicle. They may even buy your equipment for you, provide the vehicle, or fuel for the journey.

Publicity in your local area will help with sponsorship. Any unusual method of travelling between the two points may warrant publicity in national magazines or on TV. Local radio stations can be contacted to give live interviews, but set this up before you leave home.

You may find you can get blister treatments or other items you may be likely to use sponsored by chemist shops or companies.

One final word on sponsorship/publicity, you can be as successful as your imagination and determination will allow you. Think about how much you want to raise and what clothing, equipment or fuel you can get sponsored, then set about your task with enthusiasm.

When I walked I put on a t-shirt with John O'Groats to Lands End on it (photo 9) or one with the name of the charity printed on it (photo 11). I was amazed how generous people were with donations, free tea and food on route etc., particularly at roadside mobile cafes. Many people gave donations because I was wearing the t-shirt with John O'Groats to Lands End on it. If you can also put the name of a national charity on the same t-shirt then you should do even better in raising money for your charity.

FINANCIAL CONSIDERATIONS

A challenge such as this can make a sizeable hole in your pocket if you do not plan it properly. Initially you need to purchase your main equipment, boots/walking shoes/trainers, rucksack and clothing if you do not already have them. You may be able to get them sponsored either by a local shop or business or from a national supplier. This may however be difficult as national suppliers get hundreds of letters asking for equipment, so unless you can offer something different on your walk, then there is often not much chance of getting anything from them.

Once you have your equipment you need to plan how to get to John O'Groats. Haulage Company's have a network of contacts and may be able to help. So make enquiries early. I used this method with the occasional lift in a car in the more remote parts above Inverness. There are national bus companies who run buses from all over the country at least to Inverness but often to Wick, which is only 17miles from John O'Groats. There is a local bus service, which will take you to John O'Groats, but it does not run very often.

On enquiring about trains, I found that they either did not connect in Inverness at night or the cost was high compared to a coach service, and you still need to get to John O'Groats as the trains stop at Wick.

Assuming you are travelling without support, your biggest cost will be B&Bs or camping, along with food. B&Bs start at £15.00 near John O'Groats but can be as much as £35.00 in some places, especially in the south. Generally prices were around the £20.00 - £25.00 mark. I recommend carrying a small lightweight tent or a bivi

16

bag. There are places where there are no B&Bs on route or they may be full and you may need to sleep outdoors as I did six times.

You can always walk shorter distances each day and fit your schedule to where the villages are. Advantage is that you will have a good bed and shower at night, but the disadvantages are that you will often have to walk another 2 - 4miles into a village to find one and back to the main route the next day, and your overall journey will be prolonged as you are doing a lot of extra mileage.

When I walked, I stayed on the main route all the time but noted where the villages where that I would pass through and I tried to ensure I reached one before nightfall. Sometimes there were no B&Bs around at all and others were full so I used my bivi bag in a nearby field. It is important to carry one for emergency at the very least, but you may prefer to take a small tent and camp more often.

The disadvantages of staying in a B&B are that you will probably get a late start each morning from the B&B and of course the cost of staying there compared to camping. It is worth considering using B&Bs one night and camping the next.

Should you have a support team then the costs involved with that can be substantial. I travelled for most of the way without support until the latter part of the expedition. This is not a problem as long as you can wash your socks and shirt and get them dried. I attached mine to the straps on my rucksack to dry which was very effective.

Looking at food for the journey, as I stated previously, eat little and often as you walk but try where possible to have a good meal somewhere in the evening or maybe during the day. I carried fruit and bought other food on route in towns and villages etc. that I passed through. Above all, eat sensibly to maintain energy.

The above is a resumé of the main financial considerations but work your own costs out giving considerations to the above points.

THE START/FINISH

Arriving in John O'Groats, you have a beautiful view of the nearby islands. The air is clean and fresh usually with a slight wind blowing most of the time. In John O'Groats there is a tourist information centre and a café as well as a collection of small gift shops. The hotel on the front has been closed for a number of years and awaiting refurbishment although the bar on the ground floor is open.

The passenger ferry leaves from the small harbour nearby stopping off at the islands. **The last house in Scotland is nearby the harbour. In here you collect the form, which is stamped before you leave for Lands End (photo 2).** Should the shop be closed then you can collect the form from the bar in the hotel a short distance away (photo1). Try to collect your form during normal daytime hours.

The form should be stamped where possible on route to show that you stopped at places on your journey. Some receipts should be kept for B&Bs or from shops showing dates places etc, and handed in at Lands End for verification if needed.

You could not leave John O'Groats without a photograph at the signpost to record your start (photo 1). There is a similar signpost at Lands End to record your finish (photo 11). Beside the hotel is a start/finish line, finishing you cross a similar line at Lands End (photo 9).

Lands End is a tourist attraction and has many visitors. If you have a support vehicle with you, tell them to mention to the car park attendant they are doing support, and entry to the car park is free. Inside Lands End you can purchase food and drinks as well as view the attractions, which is free to 'End to Enders' finishing there.

You will see the finish line ahead as you reach the main building, **go to the post room, just inside the 'miles of memories' attraction on the right as you enter, handing in your form and receipts, if arriving at night, go to the hotel reception there.** Should you want a certificate you can purchase one by completing a form. Once you have completed the paperwork then have a tour of the site, not forgetting to have your photograph taken at the signpost before you leave.

PRACTICAL ADVICE

- Ensure you can understand and read a map well enough before you start.
- Ensure the maps used are up to date showing current roads.
- Try to plan your night stops to coincide with the B&Bs shown in this book or at villages.
- Plan a training programme; gradually increase distance and body strength.
- Ensure clothing is bright or has reflective stripes on it.
- Ensure boot/walking shoes are properly bedded in and comfortable.
- Take plenty of socks and a spare pair of trainers and change frequently.
- Take a plentiful supply of blister treatments and treat blisters promptly.
- Ensure all food, clothing and other items carried are kept to a minimum.
- If possible, have someone to meet you periodically, with clothing changes.
- Use every opportunity to replenish food and drink stocks.
- Eat little and often and drink plenty throughout the day.
- Alternate between B&Bs and bivi bag/tent if possible for a bath one day and an early start the next.
- Walk on footpaths where possible or on grass verges, only walk on roads when necessary.
- Be aware of traffic at all times from in front and from behind.
- Keep details on your person of next of kin, medical information, blood group etc. in case of accident.

THE ROUTE

You need to be familiar with the route before you leave base and I recommend studying your maps carefully. To help lighten your load, you may find it helpful to photocopy/scan the relevant sections of your intended route and carry only those pieces of route you need with you rather than numerous maps, which can be heavy.

Generally the route is well signposted throughout so you should not have much problem as long as you have a list of the road numbers to follow and towns/villages to pass through. In the route description below, I will not mention every twist and turn in the route but concentrate on the road numbers, as these are mostly signposted. I will mention some notable points on some parts of the route to help you through those parts.

Starting at the start line beside the hotel and last house in Scotland (photo 1), cross the car park then head out of **John O'Groats** on the A99 minor road, passing the Seaview Hotel and continue through **Freswick** and **Auckengill** to **Keiss,** with good views of the cliffs and headlands on route. On reaching **Reiss,** continue on the A99 to **Wick.**

Leave Wick on the A99 to pass through **Thrumster, Ulbster** and **Occumster** then **Lybster,** all of which are very small villages with no shops on your direct route, so buy what you need in Wick. When you reach **Latheron** you join the A9 which you stay on for over 100miles. In Latheron there is only a Post Office, however a little further on at **Latheron Wheel** there is a butchers and sweet shop just off the main road in the side street. There is also a steep hill to descend here.

Continuing to **Dunbeath** on the A9 there is another steep hill to descend then ascend (photo 3) then in the village there is a mini supermarket and pub a short distance away. Further on you come to **Berriedale** and the steepest hill on your journey, winding down, with a long steep ascent on the far side, it seems to take forever. The only consolation is the scenic views, monuments at the far side and a café at the bottom of the hill.

Crossing into the County of Sutherland, you descend the long winding road into **Helmsdale.** I feel that the hardest section on the whole route is between Latheron and Helmsdale as far as hills are concerned. There are shops, newsagent and a pub in Helmsdale. Ascend out of Helmsdale on the A9 and pass the villages of **Portgower** and **Loth.** You should see the sands of **Brora** in the distance and the long village there. At the far end of the village there are numerous shops and other services.

Another 9miles brings you to **Dunrobin Castle** as you enter **Golspie** and again there are a number of shops here. Walking straight through the village, continue on the A9 then cross the first of the bridges, taking you over **Loch Fleet** and down towards Dornoch. Stay on the A9 and you see the long bridge ahead crossing the **Dornoch Firth.** Take the long climb up to **Tain** where you can cut through the town and stock up on food etc as well as have a meal in the local supermarket café.

It now seems a long walk along the A9 dual carriageway to **Alness**, which is over 20miles further on. There are numerous shops in Alness and it was a recent winner of the Britain in Bloom contest. Continuing again along the A9 you arrive at a roundabout leading onto the long bridge, which takes you onto the **Black Isle.** A long 5mile climb up then down to the Tore roundabout and village and you are just 7miles from Inverness. This section can be very busy, particularly at rush hour, so try to avoid it at peak times.

Walking along the dual carriageway you come to **North Kessock,** and if you turn right down to the bottom of the road there is a mini supermarket. Beside the supermarket are some steps going up to the bridge and tourist information centre and is a small short cut.

Cross the main bridge over the **Moray Firth** to the outskirts of Inverness on the A9. Continue along this busy section then ascend the long hill to **Daviot** and the TIC there at the top. Pass **Daviot Village** then 12miles further Tomatin and the Little Chef services. This section is quite remote so have food and drink with you. Continue over **Slochd Summit** and eventually past the turn off to Aviemore, on this scenic but long route.

Arriving at **Kingussie** you can go into the village to the shops or stay on the A9 continuing to **Etteridge** then passing **Dalwhinnie** where there is only a petrol station shop in the village. Continue still on the A9 over the **Pass of Drumochter** and on to **Dalnacardoch** where you see a sign to Trinafour along a minor road to the right.

At last you are off the A9 but still in a remote area (photo 4). Follow the road into Trinafour then the signs to **Tummel Bridge** before joining the B846 to **Coshieville, Weem** then **Aberfeldy.** Cross the bridge into Aberfeldy and follow the signs through the town then along the A826 for 9miles, turning right onto the A822 to **Amulree.** It is a further 12miles to **Crieff** where there are shops to buy provisions.

Continue on the A822 through **Muthill** and **Greenloaning** just before joining the A9 dual carriageway. Take care along this busy section for the next 3½miles before branching off on the minor road, B8033 to **Dunblane.** Walk through Dunblane following signs to **Stirling** and passing through **Bridge of Allan.**

Now you are passing through a built up area, first Stirling then **St. Ninians** and on through **Bannockburn,** passing the Bannockburn visitors centre on the A872. The route passes through a section of agricultural land and runs parallel with the M80. You walk through **Dunipace** then **Denny** and on to the A80 before turning off through **Cumbernauld Village** on the A8011. Turn off again to **Luggiebank** on the B8039 then further on join the A73, which is signposted **Airdrie.** A further 3miles takes you to **Chapelhall** as you pass over the M80.

Stay on the A73 through **Wishaw** then **Carluke** and on to **Lanark** where you can obtain food and other supplies if needed. Leaving Lanark you see the first signs for Carlisle, which may motivate you, even for a short time. It seems a long way but is only 14miles from Lanark to junction 13 of the A74M where you turn onto the A702 into **Abington.**

The road now runs alongside the A74M all the way to Gretna. You pass through **Crawford, Beattock, Johnstonebridge** and **Nethercleuch.** There are virtually no shops all the way so take enough food and drink. You pass close by Lockerbie so it may be worth calling if you need supplies. Approaching the border, you pass through **Ecclefechan** and **Kirtlebridge** before reaching Kirkpatrick Fleming on the B7076.

Soon you arrive at **Gretna Green** (photo 5) and then pass through **Gretna** before walking onto the busy A74 dual carriageway. Take extra care here, staying well off the road itself. It is 6miles from Gretna, crossing the border, to **Carlisle.** Walk up the slip road off the dual carriageway and follow signs to Carlisle centre. Initially you are on the A7 then onto the A6. You are on a long straight road now for the next 15miles as you pass over the M6 at J42. Pass through **Low** and **High Hesket** then **Plumpton** before entering **Penrith.**

Photo 1
The Signpost at John O'Groats with John O'Groats hotel in the background.

Photo 2
The Author emerging from the Last House in Scotland after registration.

Stay on the A6 passing **Lowther** and going through **Shap Village** before climbing the long hill to take you over **Shap Fell.** Again stay on the A6 on the long descent to **Kendal.** Walk for 3miles on the A591 following signs for Lancaster then return onto the A6. Pass through **Milnthorpe** and **Hale** and south to **Carnforth.**

Continue to **Lancaster** where you can replenish you supplies. You have now completed the hardest half of your expedition. Now there are fewer hills, more shops and towns to buy supplies and generally more people. Stay on the A6 to go through **Garstang Village** before returning to the A6 at the far side. Your route takes you through **Preston** where you join the A49 at the far side near **Leyland** and continue through **Euxton, Coppull,** and **Standish** then into **Wigan.**

Stay on the A49 as you go through **Ashton in Makerfield** then **Newton le Willows.** Cross over the M62 then through **Warrington** and **Stockton Heath.** Continue on the A49 right down to the outskirts of **Whitchurch** then go through the town centre to rejoin the A49 on the far side. Continue on to **Shrewsbury** walking through the town centre and rejoining the A49 on the far side.

Pass through the town of **Ludlow** to again rejoin the A49 at the far side. When you reach the roundabout just before going into Leominster, turn left on the by pass and follow the signs to **Hereford** (photo 6), still on the A49. Walk through the city centre and cross the bridge over the river, following signs for Monmouth. Turn off onto the A466, 5miles past Hereford to **Monmouth.** This road is not so busy for the 18miles into Monmouth.

This next section is a winding road through dark tree lined lanes so I recommend wearing some bright clothing. When leaving Monmouth cross the A40 and onto the A466, staying on this road through **Llandogo** and passing **Tintern Abbey** before reaching **Chepstow.** You will see the **Severn Bridge** as you reach Chepstow and you continue up to the roundabout on the bridge approach road then turn left towards the bridge. Walk towards the bridge by the side of the cycle track on the left then near the bridge, go under the underpass then walk across to the right side of the bridge (photo7).

At the far side of the bridge, turn off on a path right (cutting the corner off), which brings you onto the A403. Stay on the A403 until you reach **Avonmouth** then walk under the M5 following signs to **Bristol** on the A4. This road is very busy but there is a footpath for you to walk on. Eventually you pass under the **Clifton Suspension Bridge.** Soon after, as you reach a bridge crossing the river, turn right, following signs for **Bristol Airport.** Now you turn onto the A38 and the last part of your expedition as you slowly climb up to pass Bristol Airport.

You walk through a series of small villages as you follow signs for **Highbridge** and **Bridgwater,** still on the A38. This section to Taunton is reasonably flat and you can make good progress. Continue through the centre of Bridgwater then through the village of **North Petherton,** eventually crossing the canal just before entering **Taunton.** Again, walk straight through the town centre, not round the one-way system, and return onto the A38 at the far side. You then have a 5mile section to **Wellington.**

Photo 3
One of the steep ascent and decents between Dunbeath and Helmsdale.

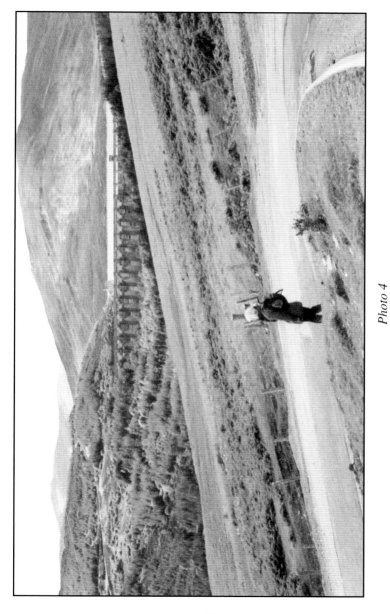

Photo 4
Walking towards Trinafour with Loch Con in the background.

Around this point the route becomes more undulating as you enter Devon, with many short but steep hills, which test your resolve. Soon you descend the A38 road to J27 of the M5 where there is a 'Little Chef' beside the roundabout. You next follow the dual carriageway, signposted to **Tiverton,** for 7miles on the A361 before turning left into Tiverton on the A396. Follow this over a series of roundabouts and follow the signs to **Crediton.** After 4miles you turn onto the A3072 to Crediton. The road between Tiverton and Crediton is extremely undulating.

Follow sign in Crediton, initially for Barnstaple on the A377 then for **Okehampton** on the A3072. You have an 18mile walk form Crediton passing through the village of **Bow** before leading on to the B3215 into Okehampton. The town has supermarkets and other shops/cafes etc where you can buy food.

Walk through the centre of Okehampton and along the B3260 towards the A30 dual carriageway, which you should see on your left. Reaching the A30, you are now on a very busy road right to Lands End, and extreme care should be taken. Wear high visibility clothing all the way to Lands End. Continue the 19miles of undulating road to by pass **Launceston** then another 22miles to by pass **Bodmin,** unless you are staying in Bodmin.

As the end is nearing, you walk on a two-way road, which is usually very busy, from SW of Bodmin to near **Indian Queens roundabout.** It is a similar route right to Penzance with dual carriageway then two-way road. Passing **Cambourne** with the monuments on the hillside off to your left, continue to Hale as you get more sea views and know the end is near. A 6mile section takes you to the outskirts of **Penzance** where you see St. Michael's Mount off to your left and the first signs to Lands End.

Arriving at the roundabout near the Tesco supermarket, still on the A30, follow the sign to **Lands End,** which is now only 12miles away. Ascend the hill there and follow the sometimes narrow, winding road where you will have your first views of the sea on both sides as you approach Lands End (photo 8). Passing through a number of small villages, you will see Lands End ahead. Walk straight to it and cross the finish line in front of the main building (photo 9).

You have finally completed your expedition (photo 10), so now go through and register your achievement in the miles of memories/post room area.

Congratulations on completing the 900 miles John O'Groats to Lands End Walk

Photo 5
A milestone on your expedition, the famous Gretna Green.

Photo 6
Entering Hereford centre just before the racecourse.

CONCISE ROUTE SUMMARY

John O' Groats – A99 ⇩
Freswick – A99
Auckengill – A99
Keiss – A99
Reiss – A99
Wick – A99
Thrumster – A99
Ulbster – A99
Occumster – A99
Lybster – A99
Latheron – A9
Dunbeath – A9
Berriedale – A9
Helmsdale – A9
Brora – A9 ⇩
Golspie – A9
Bypass Dornoch on A9
Morangie – A9
Tain – A9
Alness – A9
Tore Roundabout – A9
North Kessock – A9
Bypass Inverness – A9
Daviot – A9
Bypass Tomatin – A9
Slochd Summit – A9
Bypass Aviemore – A9
Bypass Kingussie – A9
Bypass Dalwhinnie – A9
Dalnaspidal – A9 ⇩
Pass of Drumochter – A9
Trinafour – minor road
Tummel Bridge – minor road
Coshieville – B846
Aberfeldy – B846
Amulree – A826
Crieff – A822
Muthill – A822
Greenloaning – A822
Dunblane – A9
Bridge of Allan – A9
Stirling – A9
Bannockburn – A9
Dunipace – A872
Denny – A872
Castlecary – A9/B816
Cumbernauld Village – A8011
Luggiebank – B8039
Airdrie – A73
Chapelhall – A73 ↙

Carluke – A73 ⇩
Lanark – A73
Roberton – A73
Abington – A702
Crawford – A702
Bypass Moffat – B7076
Bypass Lockerbie – B7076
Gretna Green – B7076
Carlisle – A74
Penrith – A6
Shap – A6
Kendal – A6
Milnthorpe – A6/A591/A6
Carnforth – A6 ⇩
Lancaster – A6
Garsatang Village – A6/B6430
Preston – A6
Bypass Leyland – A6/A49
Standish – A49
Wigan – A49
Ashton in- Makerfield -A49 ⇩
Newton le- Willows – A49
Warrington – A49
Stockton Heath – A49
Weaverham – A49
Whitchurch – A49
Shrewsbury town centre – A49
Church Stretton – A49
Craven Arms – A49
Ludlow town centre – A49 – minor road
Bypass Leominster – A49
Hereford town centre – A49 ⇩
Monmouth – A49/A466
Chepstow – A466
Severn Bridge – cycle path on right side.
Avonmouth – A403
Bristol – A4
Under Clifton Suspension Bridge – A4
Bristol Airport – A38
Bridgwater – A38
Taunton – A38
Tiverton – A38/A361
Crediton – A396/A3072
Okehampton - A3072/B3215 ⇩
Launceston – B3260/A30
Bypass Bodmin – A30
Bypass Camborne – A30
Penzance – A30
Lands End – A30

SUPPORT TEAM

Many people attempt this walk each year, some have full support, some partial support, and others have none. Finding someone who has the time to spare to accompany you can be a problem, but if you can find someone it can make life a lot easier. Disadvantages are the time element, the cost of accommodation and fuel for the vehicle. Advantages are that you can stop when you have had enough and be picked up as well as receive regular drinks and food on route. Best vehicles for support are a van or an estate car, which you can sleep in each night, so choose wisely.

Mobile telephones are helpful for both the support and yourself so you can keep in touch. It is easy to miss each other, especially when going through large towns or encountering vehicle one-way systems, when you can walk the direct route through a town.

Alternatively a supporter who can meet you every six days with clean clothing and food etc. is helpful, but if you have support for the whole journey then you need to ask yourself the following questions: -

1. How many people do you effectively need to give adequate support? More people means more cost, with food to provide as well as more sleeping provision?

2. What sleeping arrangements have you for the support team, camping, B&B or in the back of a van or estate car for the night?

3. Is the vehicle you are to use roadworthy for this journey and is it a thirsty one?

Photo 7
Looking back across the Severn Bridge.
From the bridge leading to the services. Your route is on the left hand side of the photograph.

38

Photo 8
The final approach.

4. Have you enough room in the vehicle for all your equipment and to spread out if you are sleeping in it?

5. Are the support team or person equipped and trained to cope with map reading and first aid as well as long days driving?

6. What facilities have you for washing/drying of everyone's clothes?

Photo 9
The finish line at Lands End, made it at last!

QUESTIONS YOU MAY ASK

How long will it take to walk and how many miles is it?
The distance is approximately 900miles, some say 910 – 960miles but as far as we know, the shortest distance is 874miles on motorways etc. Allowing for the by-roads and winding minor roads it is at least 900miles.

It will normally take about 30-60 days but it depends if you walk off route for accommodation, the weather, blisters on feet, weight of rucksack and speed of walking to name but a few. If you do it in less time then you are fit!

Are there any areas I can get lost on?
Generally the route is well signposted and if you take the route sections of map and a copy of the route described in this book then you should not have a problem. You do not need a compass. Look for the road numbers and places, if you are not sure then ask.

Is the route safe?
I found the route generally safe apart from the busy roads and the winding country lanes where you have to take extra care and try to always wear some high visibility clothing. As regards general safety, the route is no problem but always be cautious. I never had any problems on my expedition anywhere.

Which were the areas that presented most problems when walking?
The main problems I encountered were not seeing any shops where I could buy food, drinks or other items. There was not even a pub where I could obtain a meal.

This was mainly along the A9 road from Inverness right down to Aberfeldy. The section from Lanark to Abington then Crawford to Gretna Green was also short of shops, as was the A30 from Okehampton to Penzance.

You could of course walk off the main route into villages but in Scotland sometimes the villages did not even have a shop. Each time you leave your route you are walking extra miles, so decide if you are to carry a little extra food through the areas I mentioned or walk extra miles into some villages to obtain some.

The other area that presented problems was around Berriedale and generally through Scotland as regards the hills. Just before Queenswood Country Park near Hereford there's a long steep hill and around Tiverton and Crediton in Devon because of the short undulating hills. There is also the daunting Shap Fell to climb between Penrith and Kendal.

Are there plenty B&Bs on route?
No there are not many throughout the route. When starting, there are plenty in John O'Groats and Wick and generally in most villages through Scotland. There are virtually no B&Bs south of Stirling to Wishaw. Walking down the A9 there are few B&Bs unless you turn into a village.

Depending on the time of year you may find the B&Bs are full, especially in July/August. Between Crawford and Gretna there are only two or three B&Bs and from Preston to Whitchurch there was only one that I saw. Again walking along the A30 in Cornwall there was none so either be prepared to go into a village nearby or to wild camp in a field just off the road.

Photo 10
Time for photographs & celebrations.

Photo 11
The place you dream about all the way, the signpost at Lands End.

New B&Bs open as do others close, so be prepared to sleep outside. The other way is to telephone the TIC's (see appendix) throughout the route to obtain current B&B lists and pre-book all the way. The danger in doing this is that it is a long way and anything can happen with injuries, tiredness, the weather and overall fitness that may slow you down and prevent you from reaching the B&B you pre-booked.

I tried to plan to be near a village on route in the evening but it did not always work out and if there are no B&Bs for 60miles then you have no option but to sleep outside or walk off route into a village.

What should I take in terms of clothing/equipment?

The following list may help you, but each person has different requirements. **Remember when packing your rucksack that ounces turn into pounds** and rucksack straps can hurt shoulders, so choose carefully: -

1 tracksuit	Personal items
1 lightweight tent or bivi bag	Toilet paper
3 pairs of shorts (high visibility)	Notepaper/pencil
3 tops (1 long sleeve, 2 t-shirts) high visibility	Torch (small)
Water bottles (3 recommended)	4 pairs of socks
Small multiple use army knife	Camera
Mobile telephone	First aid kit
Elastic bandages/knee supports etc.	Cap/woolly hat
Sun cream/midge cream/sting relief	Cagoul/overtrousers
Travel Wash (for washing clothing)	Toiletries etc.
Survival bag/whistle	Sleeping Bag
Insect repellent	Sleep Mat?
Spare walking shoes/trainers	Food/sweets/fruit

How can I avoid blisters?

Here are some simple tips that will help you avoid blisters: -

Take plenty of socks and change them twice a day, putting talc on feet to refresh them. You will feel a lot better.

Ensure boots/trainers or walking shoes are a good fit, not too tight to cramp your feet but not too slack, otherwise feet move around and blisters form! Do not wait until you have a blister before you do something about it. Put on some moleskin, adhesive plasters, second skin or other suitable dressing as soon as you feel it rubbing or getting hot. Take a spare pair of trainers or walking shoes that you can swap around every three hours to take pressure off feet.

You could try a brand of socks called 1000-mile socks, which basically are two layers of sock that rub together instead of one layer rubbing against your skin and causing a blister. These are available from many outdoor shops.

Is the whole route on road?

Yes, it is the shortest route by road with only two small exceptions, to avoid hills or winding dangerous bends. There are some grass verges where you can walk if it has been cut short but generally you have to walk on the road or in the cycle lane at the side or on a pavement.

FIRST AID

Knowledge of basic first aid would be helpful on any
walk. Should you be unfortunate to sustain an injury then
it would be helpful if you have a first aid kit with you and
that you know how to treat your injury.

Common Types of Injuries

Cuts and grazes	*Ankle/ knee Swelling*	*Blisters*
Hypothermia	*Sprained Ankle/Wrist*	*Gashed Shins*
Shin Splints	*Bee/nettle Stings*	*Midge bites*

The above, however minor, can prove fatal, especially in an
exposed area or in times of panic, fog or adverse conditions,
coupled with the injury.

Individual First Aid Kit

Adhesive Dressing	*Blister Treatments*	*Scissors*
Triangular Bandage	*Crepe Bandage*	*Micropore*
Sterile Dressing	*Safety Pins*	*Insect Repellent*
Bandage	*Gauze/Lint*	*Sun Cream*

Hypothermia

When the body core temperature falls below 35°c if not
properly prepared for the conditions or the clothing is not
satisfactory the cold, wet, exhaustion and the wind chill
factor can cause hypothermia.

Ways of Preventing Hypothermia

1. Build up body clothing in thin layers, adding on or
   taking off as necessary.

2. Have suitable wind/waterproofs with you.
3. Eat some food/hot drink or boiled sweets, which produce energy and heat during digestion.
4. Wear a balaclava/woolly hat to insulate the head, and some gloves.
5. Shelter out of the wind.
6. Take a survival bag and if conditions dictate, use it.

APPENDIX

Tourist Information Centres on Route

John O'Groats	01955 611373
Wick	01955 602596
Dornoch	01862 810400
Inverness	01463 234353
Daviot Wood	01463 772203
Aviemore	01479 810363
Kingussie	01540 661297
Aberfeldy	01887 820276
Crieff	01764 652578
Dunblane	01786 824428
Stirling	01786 475019
Lanark	01555 661661
Moffat	01683 220620
Gretna Green	01461 337834
Carlisle	01228 625600
Penrith	01768 867466
Kendal	01539 725758
Preston	01772 253731
Wigan	01942 825677
Warrington	01925 632571
Whitchurch	01948 664577
Shrewsbury	01743 350761
Ludlow	01584 875053
Leominster	01568 616460
Hereford	01432 268430
Monmouth	01600 713899
Chepstow	01291 623772
Bristol	0906 7112191
Bridgwater	01278 427652
Taunton	01823 336344
Tiverton	01884 255827
Crediton	01363 772006
Okehampton	01837 53020
Launceston	01566 772321
Bodmin	01208 76616
Penzance	01736 362207

Distances between Towns/Villages

To find a distance, read down then right.
e.g. Dunbeath to Berriedale = 6.9miles

John O'Groats	**Miles**
⇩ to	
Freswick →	3.1
⇩ to	
Auckengill →	3.9
to	
Keiss →	2.7
to	
Reiss →	4.9
to	
Wick	2.9
Thrumpster	4.8
Latheronwheel	14.4
Dunbeath	2.9
Berriedale	6.9
Helmsdale	9.1
Brora Village (south end)	12.6
Golspie	4.8
Dornoch Firth Bridge	2.3
Alness	18.1
Cromarty Firth Bridge	5.6
Tore	5.6
Inverness Roundabout	7.6
Tomatin Services	17.4
Aviemore (north junction)	14.2
Kingussie (junction north)	14.9
Dalwhinnie (junction south)	17.3
Drumochter Summit	4.8
Trinafour	14.3
Amulree	30.2
Crieff	12.5
Braco	10.8
Dunblane (south)	9.8
Cumbernauld	23.4
Airdrie	6.6
Carluke	13.8
Lanark	5.9
Abington	19.3

Crawford	3.6
Ecclefechan	43.2
Kirkpatrick Fleming	7.5
Gretna	4.6
Longtown	3.7
Carlisle Centre	9.8
Hackthorpe	26.6
Shap	5.8
Kendal	17.7
Carnforth	12.8
Lancaster	7
Barton	20.8
Preston	5.6
Euxton	8.1
Standish Village	9
Wigan	4.1
Warrington	12.6
Stockton Heath	4.3
Whitchurch	36.4
Shrewsbury	22.3
Dorrington	7.5
Leominster	33.4
Hereford	14.7
Monmouth	20.9
Tintern Abbey	13.5
Severn Bridge (south east)	8.7
Bristol Airport	20.6
Cross village	11.8
North Petherton	20.6
Tiverton	30.9
Crediton	14.4
Okehampton	21
Bodmin	42
Victoria	8.6
Redruth (A30)	24.9
Hayle (A30)	9.4
Penzance	8
Lands End	12
Total	**900 Miles**

Bed & Breakfast Selection

The following list of B&Bs are approximately twenty to thirty miles apart, or within a days walking distance from each other. Some are slightly more due ·to shortages of B&Bs in a particular area. They have been chosen for reasonable prices, comfort and proximity to the walking route. Most are directly on the route or within a short distance from it. They are not arranged in any order of priority other than route order. Many of those listed are accustomed to having 'End to Enders' staying and they can help and advise when necessary.

You are advised to book in advance especially during main holiday times. Some B&Bs will cook evening meals so please ask when booking. To obtain further B&Bs refer to the list of T.I.C's in the appendix for the areas you require.

John O'Groats
Sea View Hotel, John O'Groats, Caithness. KW1 4YR
Tel 01955 611220
email: seaviewhotel@barbox.net
www .johnogroats-seaviewhotel.co.uk

Wick
Harbour Guest House, 6 –7 Rose St, Wick. KW1 5EX
Tel 01955 603276

Berriedale On the main route through Berriedale
Mrs Gough, Kingspark Llama Farm, Berriedale,
Caithness. KW7 6 HA
email: MryGough@aol.com
www.llama.plus.com

Golspie
Mrs J. Payton, Rhives House, Golspie, KW10 6SD
Tel. 01408 633587

Tain
Dunbius Guest House, Morangie Rd,
Tain Ross-shire. IV19 1HP
Tel. 01862 894902
email: rogermach@aol.com

Inverness This B&B is in the centre of Inverness
near the castle.
Jean & Tony Gatcombe, Ardmuir House, 16 Ness Bank,
Inverness. IV2 4SF
Tel/Fax: 01463 231151
e-mail: hotel@ardmuir.com
www.ardmuir.com

Tomatin ¾mile up lane. Turn to Tomatin at the Little
Chef then right then left at Silver Birches house.
Glenan Lodge Guest House, Tomatin,
Inverness-shire. IV13 7YT
Tel 01808 511217
www.glenanlodge.co.uk

Kingussie This B&B is situated approx. 200yds
off the A9 first turning left towards Kingussie
then left again.
A free massage is available!
The Auld Poor House, Kingussie. PH21 1LS
Tel 01540 661558
email: gordon@yates128.freeserve.co.uk
www.yates128.freeserve.co.uk

Aberfeldy
48 The Lees, Dunkeld St, Aberfeldy. PH15 2AF
www.leesaberfeldy.btinternet.com

Crieff
The Carrick, 57 Burrell St, Crieff. PH7 4DG
Tel. 01764 656595
www.thecarrick.co.uk

Stirling Near Bannockburn Heritage Centre.
Cambria Guest House, 141 Bannockburn Rd,
Stirling. FK7 0EP
Tel. 01786 814603
www.visitbannockburn.com

Airdrie On B803 at Glenmavis north of Airdrie.
Rowan Lodge, 23 Condorrat Rd, Glenmavis,
Airdrie. ML6 0NS
Tel. 01236 753934
www.rowanlodge.com
email: june@rowanlodge.com

Wishaw
Herdshill Guest House, 224 Main St, Bogside,
Wishaw. ML2 8HA
Tel 01698 381579

Lanark On route
Summerlea, 32 Hyndford Rd, Lanark. ML11 9AE
Tel. 01555 664889

Crawford On route
Holmelands Country House, 22 Carlisle Road,
Crawford. ML12 6TW
Tel. 01864 502753
www.holmlandscotland.co.uk
email: dan.Davidson@holmlandscotland.co.uk

Beatock Beside roundabout at J.15
Lochhouse Farm Retreat Centre, Beatock. DG10 9SG
Tel. 01683 300451
email: martin@lochhousefarm.com
www.lochhousefarm.com

Lockerbie Cross motorway bridge on the Dumfries Rd, 400yds on right.
The Elms, Dumfries Rd, Lockerbie. DG11 2EF
Tel. 01576 203898
www.theelms-lockerbie.com
email: enquiries@theelms-lockerbie.com

Gretna Green Close to Station.
Kirkcroft Guest House, Glasgow Rd,
Gretna Green. DG16 5DU
Tel. 01461 337 403
www.kirkcroft.co.uk
email: info@kirkcroft.co.uk

Carlisle Near bus and railway station in centre.
Cornerways Guest House, 107 Warwick Rd,
Carlisle. CA1 1EA
Tel. 01228 521733

Penrith
Anne Ross, Thrimby Farm, Thrimby,
Penrith CA10 3DY
Tel 01931 712484
email: rross@ktdinternet.com

Shap On route
Fell House, Main St, Shap, Cumbria. CA10 3NY
Tel. 01931 716343
www.shapaccommodation.co.uk
email: fellhouse@btopenworld.com

Kendal On route
Glenholme Guest House, 43 Milnthorpe Rd,
Kendal. LA9 5QG
Tel. 01539 721489
email: glynis@glenholme43.freeserve.co.uk

Carnforth On A6

Dale Grove, 162, Lancaster Rd, Carnforth LA5 9EF

Tel. 01524 733382

www.dalegrove.co.uk

email: stevenage@ntlworld.com

Bilsborrow Nth of Preston On A6

Olde Duncombe House, Garstang Road, Bilsborrow,
Preston. PR3 0RE

Tel 01995 640336

email: oldedunc@aol.com

Charnock Richard On Route

Hinds Head Hotel, Preston Rd, (A49),
Charnock Richard, Chorley. PR7 5HL

Tel. 01257 791365

email: hazelhindshead@aol.com

Warrington Near A49 (south)

New House Farm Cottage, Hatton Lane, Hatton,
Warrington. WA4 4BZ

Tel. 01925 730567

Whitchurch Just off town centre.

Mrs. D. Clubbe, Pheasant Walk, Terrick Road,
Whitchurch, Shrop. SY13 4JZ

Tel. 01948 667118

Shrewsbury. South of town. Situated off main road ¾
mile on right, up lane.

Mrs. D Farmer, Chatford House, Bayston Hill,
Nr Shrewsbury.

Tel 01743 718301

Church Stretton
Rheingold, 9, The Bridleways,
Church Stretton. SY6 7AN
Tel. 01694 723969

Ludlow
The Mount, 61 Gravel Hill, Ludlow,
Shropshire. SY8 1QS
Tel 01584 874084
Email: rooms@themountludlow.co.uk

Hereford 5 minutes from Cathedral in centre.
Bouvrie Guest House, 26 Victoria St,
Hereford. HR4 0AA
Tel. 01432 266265

Monmouth Free pick up drop off service.
Mrs. E Alcock, Casita Alta, 15 Toynbee Close,
Osbaston, Monmouth. NP25 3NU
Tel. 01600 713023 Mob. 0775 9074808
email: bb.alcock@btopenworld.com

Chepstow Just off roundabout on route.
Valerie Kells, Lower Hardwick, Hardwick Hill,
Chepstow. NP16 5PT
Tel. 01291 620515
email: valeriekells@valeriekells.fsnet.co.uk

Highbridge 200yds off A38
Sandacre, 75 Old Burnham Rd, Highbridge,
Somerset. TA9 3JG
Tel. 01278 781221

Taunton
Brookfield Guest House, 16 Wellington Rd,
Taunton.TA1 4EQ
Tel. 01823 272786
www.brookfieldguesthouse.uk.com
email: info@brookfieldguesthouse.uk.com

Tiverton In Town Centre.
Tony Evans, The Angel Guest House, 13 St. Peters St,
Tiverton. EX16 6NU
email: cerimar@eurobell.co.uk

Crediton Near railway station.
Mrs. S. Pugsley, Great Park Farm, Crediton. EX17 3PR
Tel. 01363 772050
email: susan.pugsley@virgin.net

Okehampton On Route.
Meadowlea Guest House, 65 Station Road,
Okehampton. EX20 1EA
Tel. 01837 53200

Launceston
Glencoe Villa, 13, Race Hill, Launceston. PL15 9BB
Tel 01566 775819/773012
email: <keigil.robinson@virgin.net>

Bodmin
Elm Grove, 2 Elm Grove, Cardell Road,
Bodmin. PL31 2NJ
Tel. 01208 74044   Mob. 07929 922047

Redruth Near Railway Station.
Nina & Robert Giles, 42 Clinton Rd,
Redruth. TR15 2QE
Tel. 01209 216002
email: lansdowne@ziplip.com
www.lansdowne-guesthouse.co.uk

Penzance
Lynwood Guest House, 41, Morrab Rd,
Penzance.TR18 4EX
Tel. 01736 365871
email: lynwoodpz@aol.com
www.lynwood-guesthouse.co.uk

Main Towns/Villages on Route

John O' Groats
Wick
Helmsdale
Brora
Golspie
Inverness (just off)
Aviemore (just off)
Kingussie (just off)
Aberfeldy
Crieff
Dunblane
Stirling
Denny
Cumbernauld
Airdrie
Lanark
Lockerbie (just off)
Gretna
Carlisle
Penrith
Kendal
Lancaster

Preston
Wigan
Warrington
Whitchurch
Shrewsbury
Ludlow
Leominster (just off)
Hereford
Monmouth
Chepstow
Bristol
Bridgwater
Taunton
Tiverton
Crediton
Okehampton
Launceston (just off)
Bodmin (just off)
Redruth (just off)
Hayle (just off)
Penzance
Lands End

Useful Addresses

Lands End - John O'Groats End to End Club
The Customs House
Lands End
Penzance
Cornwall TR19 7AA
Tel 01736 871501
Email: info@landsend-landmark.fsnet.co.uk
Cilla George (home email): cillageorge@aol.com
Advice and information, magazines and special offers for
club members.

Long Distance Walkers Association
Les Maple
21 Upcroft, Windsor, Berks. SL4 3NH
Tel. 01753 866685
This association is set up to further the interests of those who enjoy long distance walking. Members receive a journal three times each year, which includes information on all aspects of long distance walking.

Ramblers Association
2nd Floor, Camelford House,
87-90 Albert Embankment, London SE1 7TW
Tel. 01577 861222
Advice and information on all walking matters.
Local groups, regular meetings.

The route described in this book was the one used by the author in 2003 and believed to be correct at the time of publication. Hopefully you have enjoyed this walk and gained as much pleasure from walking the route as he did. Should you wish to walk another route, please visit Challenge Publications website at: -

www.chall-pub.fsnet.co.uk

A wide selection of walking guides covering the UK are available including 'The National Three Peaks Walk'. The top selling book covering the famous three peaks routes and containing everything you need to know to complete the challenge.

On our website you will find other interesting, and possibly different walks around the British Isles, which are equally as picturesque and enjoyable as this one.

Should you wish to comment on this book or give further information to help keep the book updated then please write to the address below or e-mail via the website. An acknowledgement will be given: -

Please write to: -
Challenge Publications
7, Earlsmere Drive, Ardsley, Barnsley. S71 5HH

John O'Groats to Lands End Expedition Diary

Use the following pages to record your experiences, highs and lows of your walk. You should include the following on a daily basis.
1. Weather
2. Start/Finish Times
3. Distance Walked
4. Overnight Stay
5. From/To
6. Special Points

Day 1. _____

_____

_____

_____

_____

_____

_____

_____

_____

_____

_____

_____

_____

_____

_____

_____

_____

_____

_____

_____